OPPOSITES

Written by A.J. Wood
Illustrated by Helen Ward

PRICE/STERN/SLOAN
Publishers, Inc., Los Angeles
1987

HAPPY!
A happy hyena
laughs at...

SAD!
a sad gorilla.

**FAST!
A fast antelope
leaps over...**

SLOW!
a slow tortoise.

TIMID!
A timid wombat
hides from...

FIERCE!
a fierce leopard.

WET!
A wet crocodile
smiles at...

DRY!
a dry rhino.

CLEAN!
A clean zebra
stares at...

DIRTY!
a dirty pig.

THIN!
A thin snake
slithers past...

FAT!
a fat hippo.

SMOOTH!
A smooth koala
talks to...

PRICKLY!
a prickly porcupine.

ASLEEP!
A fast asleep sloth
hangs next to...

AWAKE!
a wide awake owl.

BIG!
A big elephant
makes friends with...

LITTLE!
a little mouse.